CAPTAIN CAPTIONS CANADA

KEN KEITH NAKAMURA

authorHOUSE®

AuthorHouse™
1663 Liberty Drive
Bloomington, IN 47403
www.authorhouse.com
Phone: 1 (800) 839-8640

Published by AuthorHouse 02/21/2017

ISBN: 978-1-5246-7234-8 (sc)
ISBN: 978-1-5246-7233-1 (e)

Print information available on the last page.

Any people depicted in stock imagery provided
by Thinkstock are models, and such images are
being used for illustrative purposes only.
Certain stock imagery © Thinkstock.

This book is printed on acid-free paper.

Because of the dynamic nature of the Internet,
any web addresses or links contained in this book
may have changed since publication and may no
longer be valid. The views expressed in this work are
solely those of the author and do not necessarily
reflect the views of the publisher, and the publisher
hereby disclaims any responsibility for them.

BIOGRAPHY

My name is Ken Keith Nakamura.

My collection of captions for the groundwork of Captain Captions begun in 1975. After 5 and 6 years of university and college I started as an occasional teacher with the TDSB. Toronto District School Board. I am in my initial 37th year as supply teacher with TDSB. I have a BA from York 1979 and a Law Certificate from Centennial College 79 and 80 and a BED OTC from University of Toronto 1980-81.

I have 2 daughters, twins and a step daughter who I have not seen in 15 years.

The name of the book is Captain Captions Canada by Ken Keith Nakamura.

Preamble to the Book

The book can be made into a game like verbal sudoku. Each page has playing cards and a blank for the players of the game to:

A. Read orally in seminar form
B. Make your own captions
C. Make your own advertisement game. Or make your own advertisement using your own prose or caption
D. Make your own speech based on a few of Captain Captions prose and your own
E. Make a debate using your captions or one of my captain captions
F. Make up notes of the book
G. Take one of my playing cards, one of my captain captions and for the artists in you, make a pictograph picture out of the caption. Make some art from the words. Have fun. Make art from poetry
H. Make up charades out of my captions
I. Make up a song about your prose

Hay BEER	Dreams compromise reality
The Bear store	A Spiderman in every closet
Charming Hors d'oeuvres Cowabuggle	Salary Celery Missed by a country's centimeter
Frustration and development	Shades of the paragraph
Aurora Borealis of the Galaxies The Arrogant forgave	Note of the counsellor. Duty Notes.

Arithmetic of Grammar Mathematics of Language.	Poetic Legislation
Faults are eroded by their strengths.	Eucharistic Euchre
A camera is a press release.	The simplicity of excellence
Children are the movie stars of winter. They leave there footprints in the snow.	The hills were as grey as the sky as the snow lightened the day

A.M. Activists	We are cut from the same clothing Christmas is a slack day
PM'S Sandwich	Hamsters jogging
Dishes Two Lemon thumbs up We are optimistic about eternal Peace	Chores of inspiration
Sorrow dispense evil	Play doh Crusades
Muskie Muskeg	Piano of the log cabin

The hour of the subconscious.	Fear embodies guilt and guilt embodies discipline
Qualitative approach to labor Qualitatively	A baseball players hand that turned to leather.
Right as paint	Patient as a dentist
Semantics of Physics	MILKY WAY THE NIGHT SKY The PROUD BANNER OF ASTRONOMY The stars the police officers of the ghost of the Milky Way

Fruits of the labor movement Optimism	The Clause of Integrity
Disclaimer a tribute	Man the amendment
Layman's Mayhem	Anonymous Maple Leaf sayings
Prose that does not leave a mark	Fussy Creativity Defeat of Patriotism

Objectives are treasures	Crayons and the chipmunk
Workaholic Canoe	Nato singers
There's a caramelized trout at the end of a rainbow	Musical talk
Making a useful difference	A good question is a comment and or commentary and or open promise

Walk like a hike	Staggering author
Library juke box	The Dewey decimal point of publishing and broadcasting
Peanuts for potatoes	On the porch you say tomato we say potato
The grate Potato	Cats in the dog house

The Beavers Igloo		Shopping for Utopia	
Cattle Cross		The Haggis where you still taste the bagpipes	
The bell curve of Sergeant computer		All FEET ON DECK Desire Celibacy	
Our era has begun		The DESSERT SIDEWALKS AND WINDOWS OF OUR GREAT CONURBANE Nation	

Gopher Broke	Progress is an example of the Tabula Rasa
Redundant as an Xylophone	Mayors of Altruism
Chopstick on the Accordion	Maximum Empathy
Compact Gear	Novelty of goodwill
The HONEST DOLLAR Snack economy	The welfare of fraud Camping on mosquito disorder Cold and proud

Trail to the room	Honor Humor
Language is impressive	Man is the partner of the creator
Icicles and manners	The pause between God and man
A poor man's snowman on a millionaire's toboggan	Scrooge Writers
Razor blade hockey and skating	Elastic geometry
Humorous Chromosome	Brave brain

Odyssey of snowfall	Peas for peace
Canada the land of ice and snow where the ancient winds blow and the rain is a white as snow	A halibut of a great potato
Rain makes you stronger	Canadian Cosmopolitan A great conservative 7 in the morning and 332 PM.
Giraffe graphing	A clean mark
You grow like a graph	Rivera ravine look
Yoga Yogurt	Inflation of the balloon

Further than further	Cheerleading politics. The Political schoolhouse
Bongo Command	Bleachers of the lecture
Better half of the plate	Clean manure
Lackadaisical lactose	Relief belief
Oscar KABOSA	Older the order
Glide calories	Raining like Gods pee

Golden memoirs	Vitamin cellar
No beans no means	Serious silly clock
Our product is job satisfaction	Engine of the journal
Jingle jungle	Honor roll of attendance
Patterns of successful themes	Eventually ethical
Heart like a gear	Cliff hanger coat hanger

Mug warming cafe	Full as toast
Quaker before the Lord and his oatmeal song	Shotgun of the bong
A glass of cold cow	Cooking like coaching
Resume grows	Dribble dabble
Great scholarship arrives at the door of the abyss	Meal presentation is everything next to hunger

Whistling ravens	Shear kilt
Girdle guarders	Question and privilege of fairness
Loafing around the flour mill	Puck eclipse
Chalkboard Mandate	Commissioner of pins and buttons.
Mushrooming of human rights	Proud metal

Sergeants computer	Ties as fatigues
Jealous pimples	Love creates art and art creates an image that is a representative or representation of reality
Amber red and green patterns of successful themes	Natural teachings
Success is measured by effort	Appearance of brilliance
Tales of wildlife	Generous genius
Poetic medication that footnotes the world	Poetic legislation

Fictional confessions	Balanced growth
Your hands are nude	Tuba band
Legal acts of literature	Work as a savings
Survival with momentum	Early and smart The early round robin gets the worms
Normal anticipation	God as a psychiatrist
Watermelon fountain	Camp ivy mosquitoes

We are billions of years away from the beginning of time Alliance	Daily tribulations and joy clues of the good Afterlife
Reincarnated voice stomachs Paramecium Gland	Ammo food
Who has seen the window	Mature nature
The bay of funding	Mature nature
Close as a cigar	Thinking around the circle A sing song
Spoon then the shovel	Explanation of cleaning

Malice of a mallard.	The democracy of television
Motown hood	Acceptable respectable and approved
Alkaline names	Amen burning with corn Flakes
Biology skits	Utterance extinction
Info guns	The democracy of television
Cattle army	Labs to restaurants

Good deeds that multiply	Dinosaur teeth and gypsy feet
Good schooling is like a regiment without a rank	Industrial recreation and the Kleenex of sports
Remembrance of the cattle axe	Glacial pyramids of our governing bodies
Stockyard DNA and our great ancestors	The world and our local is our jury of our collective happiness

Thick plate Paper chefs The more you clean the more you cook a clean plate means dessert	Cookie pills
Serenade of salutations All - star activities	Optimistic about perpetual peace. Shut the well up
The umbrella fell and elastic geometry Axiom of affiliation and associations	Bagel Sunday Born again steaks
Waiting on exceptional answers and there profound genesis Accountability and the evidence	Traffic poet Prince charming in the drink.
Mellow colors. Gullible lollipops The box of soccer	Hurdle the turtle
River Applause The Children and the community are the homegrown peace keepers of our great nation	Snakes ladder. The worms

Ken Keith Nakamura

Advertising. The Evolution of the syllogism.	Powerful comfortable prayers makes for a comfortable conscience The resume grows
Playing the drama. Empress panda bear and Santa Claus Haiku galaxy	The Innocence of loss. Elusive equity
Doodling economists The Granite trees of Autumn stick out like paint brushes and they say paint me paint me	Maximum empathy.
Vegetable insulation The butchers holiday	Halitosis mitosis Onion Visine
School is like a book that never closes	Bambi archery
Church and the garage	Plasma breath Friends are as regular as good pie
Hockey night in Hollywood	Snow clouds where the winter galaxies are.

Speechmaker Making a bag of goodies in a time of crisis.	Science and pollution
Puzzle of confusion Manifestations of manifestos	The failure of writing and the success of man
Institutions are manmade mountains	The city is my country home
The spotlight is on our exceptional students and staff	The love of work. Working is fun
Instant lamb stew	Vulnerability of humanity

The Democracy of television	Make a light bulb using mirrors
Content makes its own message	Winter personalities and ethics. Motors the guitars
Good broadcasting and Journalism is like a good medium steak	Straws for cows Nuclear family Pluto Plutonium Uranus Uranium and Mercury Pressure
Faith Swimming	50 cows equals 100 desserts
Charcoal ribs Boogie	Colonel clerk. The GENERAL SECRET

Anthem prayer	Humidity perseverance. Sustenance in Appetite
Bourgeoisie cheese	The depression Of ambition
Latent compliments	Granny Smith Smiley faces
Grinning grape fruit breakfast Vinegar bouquet of the wine	Guilty tummy
Navy nose Faster than mistakes slower that the flow	Landscape Architects The BRIDGE HOME

The moon is as white as a snowball a soccer ball a golf ball a baseball a ping pong ball	Newtonian balls Ballpoint swords
Electrifying the airplane and aero space industry	Factory funny
Philippines cream cheese of Philadelphia Powerful barbers and coffers	Gondola with the wind
Windy the sailors girlfriend	Popular as a sailor
Mouse of the moose	Elaine the bowler's girlfriend. Canon ball bowling without the fodder

Adequate improvement of the intellect.	Einstein and Aristotle are students of modern man
Prisoner of history Recycling plant	The earth is the center of the big bang
Anchor of geography	Skinny milk
Granite trees	There's sustenance in appetite

Behind every word a story	Bow to the arrow
Alphabet accountants	Our flag salutes our children when they are at ease
Don't choke on the artichoke.	The Bayonet knife of gastronomy
Tears of the stomach	The power of safety and the luxury of health

Assisting the successful. Safe entertainment. Making a safe environment	Flush your friends make way for your co workers
Editors of the bar	Victory in reason
The audience is your friend	Biking like shinny hockey
Success of worrying	Jet to cave
Proud animals wait	All feet on deck Desire celibacy

The Era has begun	Certified fulfillment
Steps of the next decade	Caricature of juxtapositions
The nib of metaphysics touching the first metaphor	Bomb every city with amended legislation
Presbyterian like pedestrians	Stable fame
Dinosaur teeth	Non prolific beaches

Seamless knowledge is acknowledgement.	Conjuring up conjugations
Elastic geometry	The confident Laureate directing leadership
Epistemology pedagogy and curriculum	Tracing the landscape
Threw the snowball effect	Fight at doing your job right
Beefing up the poems	A foreign tomorrow

COSMOS GENDER	A WHALE TOMORROW
Elucidated carbon	There enough salad to feed an army of Canada's moose
Merit race the face of the race	The Coefficient of context
Critique improvements and consistency	The power of the sword and the prosperity of power
Indoor rain outdoor characters	Praise the food
Tourists intelligences	Banjo wife

Pilgrim saturations	Social justice diversification
Deaf apologies	Committees communion
Negotiating nursery rhymes and the inequities in your daily contract	Naturally tasteless you're a cliché
Accolades of risk	Bourgeoisie cheese
The odyssey of snow. Canuck Snowflakes	The web of free will

Redressing in the shadows	The individual as the collective
Proper numbers behave Improper slurring numbers misbehave	Snoring a teardrop
Fairness of literature	Testament of the fridge
A strikes decimal point	Minutes of the revolution
The veil of the treble clef	The coefficient of context

Freedom in stress	The pause between God AND MAN
The UNKNOWN GOOD	Emotive language is the roots of our laws
Content makes its own message	White light of dentine
You're a giant to your childhood	Ornaments of religions
Giant mom	Dethroning a regime every May

Developing a criminals conscience to his demise	An excellent attitude is an achievement
Therapy writing	Folks of the union spokes
Your words are on fire	OINK GOES THE PEN
Tip of the ice cube	Preservation and conservation a natural motive
Epigrams that exonerate you	Thunder over the puddle
Noble flexibility	When your river is down and out

Natures fascism	Frogsaurus cowasaurus
The lakes blow up	The Right Honorable patience
Salute your hands on organization	Urban isolation
Labor arrived at the door of bureaucracy	Solitude the hands of the clock away
The expert of existence and essentialism	We are above the water and the land

The guns of the free world unite	Cowboys and popcorn
Guns are junk built by the museum	Scribble talking
Healthy habits	Barbecue clouds
Alphabet accountants	Legal bells erasing wonder
The Indescribable sky	A classroom is an ethical stimulus
Slapstick drama and chopstick phrases	

Anonymous Maple leaf sayings	Logic grammar
Canadian fire Camp maple leaf flag burning. The red embers	Church building. the woodworkers sermon
Manifest graffiti	Canadian Nationalism The DRUMMER IS IDLE a COUNTRY'S NATIONALISM
Sap Engineering	Limonene politicians
REVIVAL. Vitalization of man animal and machine and music	The RIVALRY TEAM
Religious politicians	Spiritual cholesterol

Rubrics ease	Marmalade and steaks
The happy ruler Trouble shooting that does not cost money	Beyond categorization
Put a muffler on your diatribe.	Open and closed reading
Open and Closed reading	Stay tuned for comic identification
Pragmatically tired	MYTHS OF THE LEGENDS Rural and urban

Natural and artificial	Perceived products
Respect in indifference	Philosophical breakthroughs
Touch electricity	Respect in neutrality Truck drivers domain and in reservation
The failure of capitalism and the advent of breakfast	Polident toothpaste and fluoride bubblegum
Faster than mistakes slower than the flow	Pyramid of memory

Altos of the workplace	Script of the psyche
Factor actor	A good meal is like a pill of good health
Windpipe flute	Surfacing and leaving the lake
Oracle of the edible	Visine onions
The friendship of Independence	Terminal grazing

To a point Arrogance breeds equality	Waiting in line of the nation's builders,	Nasal Damsel
Alkaline names are used to make a better world	Play on the going and the waiting	The cattle's military academy
Spud fish A halibut of a potato	The Pronoun I and Number 1 The glucose girl	
Shark tuna sandwich	The Prairie lakes blow up and rumble	
Rank philanthropy	Chopsticks on the accordion	
The Cadillac castles of the neighborhood	Piano of the log cabin	

Emperor panda honey bamboo Use your utilities	What the international chair said to the global pupils Your desk is the best
Bowing Protestants and Catholics Mom is a giant Class ibid	A cows soldier A whale of hardships
Perfect behavior inspires	Teaching is an innovation and an Activity
Crayons and the chipmunk	YOU'RE A GIANT TO YOUR CHILDHOOD
Prose establishes corporations	There's more in the process than the product
Hero zero	Reality over fiction. confessions

Arbitrations victorious window	The Constitution of linguistics
8 billion ghosts	Winter weather is a polar bear fridge
The bell curve of sergeants computer	Perfume sausages
Paint yourself into the boat	Speechless for a remedy

Property hooks	Less is more
Predicting the constellations and using the gender astrology to plot a course	When ideas become ideology
Full pork and stork ahead	Fiction is on the road home to reality. What counts
All of man's sorrow a woman's makeup tomorrow	Tangible gifts.

Baptize the boat	Bullet of contraband
Photon photos	Cranberries giving thanks everyday
Sticking the decree of the plumbers throne	Your week as an astronaut
Beware of the dog of 2020	The vitamin cellar

The magnificence of Algonquin and the pyramids	Do not disturb charades
Private public PUB guidelines	GROUP HIERARCHY YOUR INVITATION OF YOUR PERSONAL PROSPECTUS
Intermediate mentoring GRADE A RESOLUTIONS	SPEED UP COMPREHENSIONS
THE BEST DEN AND HARP	Fluoride ice cream 8 billion ghosts

The right honorable patients	Pierogi Prerogative
The mosque in bloom	The frogs' ribbiting was righteous
Sleeping imitates playing	Smiling statues
Laugh, it's uphill	Rameses' cat Lancelot
Your works compliment you	The gifted helping the struggle

Printed in the United States
By Bookmasters